Wicked Waves

Tabitha Parker Mendez

Presentation by *BookLeaf Publishing*

Web: www.bookleafpub.com

E-mail: info@bookleafpub.com

ISBN: 9789394788923

First edition 2022

DEDICATION

K.A.M

PREFACE

Behold, the dark triad.

Built of three sides, narcissism, machiavellianism and psychopathy. Behold the dark triad.

My great grandmother would always share words from the wise. I could never quite understand who these "wise" men were, or why they had such silly advice.

Now I understand. I understand just how those men became so wise.

She would say if something doesn't feel right, it probably isn't. I had a feeling that something wasn't right.

Something was terribly wrong, and in time I would learn exactly just how terrible.

The truth always reveals itself. Another tale from the wise men. Followed by the truth will set you free.

I need to be free, I need to tell the truth.

My Haiku

Tabitha Marie,

Lady of the bitter sea,

C'est la vie, said she.

The Target

He chose me because I was weak. I was vulnerable. I was a victim.

I had just barely begun standing on two feet. The aftermath of my husband's absence was gut wrenching and life altering. Betrayal has returned, this time with a new name. I don't want to play this game, not now. Not again.

I need to get out of here, I cannot explode. He follows me towards my rogue, lying through his teeth. I spin around, keys gripped in my fist, colliding with the window of her car; glass shattered down like a waterfall.

Just get back to work, just breathe and drive. In through the nose, out through the mouth. You just have to make it back to the restaurant.

My ride from his driveway to the restaurant was silent. I didn't notice the blood right away, but the warm drops flowed down my fingers and my hand felt wet. Don't look. Don't look.

The restaurant had been my home base, the kitchen a place to feel safe and place to vent. The staff had welcomed me there with open arms. A feeling much needed in the years of torment. It was my place of refuge.

"Where's Chef?!" I yell shakily. I head straight for the sink and ask for the first aid supplies. Bloody hand, "I think that there's glass in my knuckles."

Sobbing in the restaurant kitchen, I bandaged my hand and took a shot of tequila.

Chef barrels around the corner, "What the fuck happened?!" My adrenaline is wearing off. Between sobs I managed to explain that after finding another woman that I considered a friend, in the driveway of my lover's home, things began to unfold.

The confrontation was over within minutes, but not without destruction.

A post traumatic ghost of my past arrives with dread. How can this be happening? She was supposed to be a friend. I knew something wasn't right. After all, a wiseman once said the gut doesn't lie.

It was my own personal twilight zone. A series of unfortunate events tell the story of my life. Yet after each unfortunate blow, my soul breathes a whisper of hope. The last battlefield has cleared out.

Rage and despair take control and all I can see is the bottomless black hole. Barely standing at the edge, the narcissist is ready. A silent hunter waiting for the right moment with the right victim.

Target in sight.

Noch, aim, loose.

Bullseye.

Narcissistic Eyes

5

I saw the darkness in his eyes, but I wasn't afraid. I was intrigued. What is his darkness trying to hide?

Like a shadow lingering behind, he watched. He watched everything. He watched everyone. He watched me.

Anxiety replaces my curiosity; the eyes I was once so in love with now belong to my worst enemy.

I can feel them in the shadows. Rage and fury glowing.

He drops hints and cues. Methodical and personal, the narcissist needs me to know. He will never leave me alone.

Capture The Flag

Tricked into playing his game,
he always had the lead.
Warning signs everywhere,
I chose not to read.

I stumbled through hopeful and optimistic,
tripped into sadness and confusion.
Down the hill of rage and anger,
landing in a hollow hole of despair.

No Tune

As the story unfolds,
I can see the pain,
taking its toll.

Darkness rapidly
taking control.

We have lost the chance,
of true loves dance.
For a heart without a beat,
holds no tune.

Silence,
much too soon.

Wicked Waves

Gone are the days,
the sun warmed her bones.

Lightning strikes ashore,
blinding bolt to the core.

A familiar storm,
she's been here before.

Flame

Blazing fire,

Eye to eye,

Burning desire.

Heads or Tails?

Gaslight,
green light.

Gatekeeper,
truth seeker.

Girlboss,
coin toss.

Midnight Cries

Years of salty tears,
Anguished cries,
Towards the midnight skies.

Enemies in disguise,
True love is blind,
From the ashes...

A Phoenix will rise.

Chaos

Drowning in chaos,
She is lost.

Cursed with an eternity,
Of pain and agony.

Clarity

There's truth within every lie.
His jealous insecurities,
Would only provide the clarity.

Strumming his guitar,
To confident behind,
His intricate and clever lies.

Bold and malicious,
Twisted and sadistic.
Begging forgiveness,
Proclaiming innocence.

Pyre

Haven't you a chance to learn?

I'm a witch baby.

I ain't afraid to burn.

Haiku #2

15

The weeping willow.

The green grass, mellow meadows.

The wild sea waves crash.

Monster Within

It pains me to see
You so uncomfortable in your own skin.

The lies and deceit
Eat you from within.

Mirrors of pain
Nothing to gain.

Cancer ●

Battle after battle,
Red crab,
Rages in vain.

So much to lose,
So much to gain.

Flees shore to shore,
Desperate to seek,
A victorious gain.

Crave

Our love has been sentenced to die,
A future sealed by fate.

Underground,
Buried alive.

The flickering light of hope,
Begins to choke.

Gone out,
With a cloud of smoke.

Desperate for your touch,
I crave one more hug.

Split

There was good in him,
This I have seen.

Piercing through,
His eyes of green.

Anger and hatred,
Boiled within.

Weaves a wicked web,
Of lies and deceit.

A mask no more,
Split core.

Haiku #3

This is destiny,

My soul crying out to me,

This is victory.